Published by Sterling Publishing Co., Inc.
387 Park Avenue South, New York, NY 10016

Distributed in Canada by Sterling Publishing
c/o Canadian Manda Group, 165 Dufferin Street,
Toronto, Ontario, Canada M6K 3H6

Distributed in the United Kingdom by GMC Distribution Services,
Castle Place, 166 High Street, Lewes, East Sussex, England BN7 1XU

Distributed in Australia by Capricorn Link (Australia) Pty. Ltd.
P.O. Box 704, Windsor, NSW 2756, Australia

ISBN 13: 978-1-4027-3897-5
ISBN 10: 1-4027-3897-8

Printed in China

10 9 8 7 6 5 4 3 2 1

For information about custom editions, special sales, premium and
corporate purchases, please contact Sterling Special Sales
Department at 800-805-5489 or specialsales@sterlingpub.com.

Sterling Publishing Co., Inc.
New York

Celebrating
Snow Globes

By Nina Chertoff and Susan Kahn

Introduction

Today the world is filled with snow globes, and snow globes are filled with the world. Like magic, with a quick flip of the wrist, a snow globe will create a charming little scene that transports you somewhere else—if only for a moment.

The snow globes that we see most often today are tourist souvenirs, wonderful remembrances of the trip to Colonial Williamsburg or the family reunion in Kansas City. But in their early heyday, snow globes were associated with true romance. After all, they were created by the French—derived, most likely, from the process used to create glass paperweights. The first snow globe to attain widespread attention depicted one of the most romantic sites in the world—Paris's Eiffel Tower. Introduced at the Paris Exposition in 1889, it was a great success.

It wasn't long before snow globes seemed to capture the imagination of everyone, and as their popularity spread, they were manufactured in many European countries. German companies began exporting them to the United States in the 1920s, where they were quickly appreciated.

An American entrepreneur, Joseph Garaja of

This lovely depiction of the Eiffel Tower was the first snow globe to attract widespread attention.

Pittsburgh, Pennsylvania, began to produce snow globes in the late 1920s, and while he had a patent, it didn't seem to protect his creations from being copied. Soon many companies were making them. Early ones were used not only to advertise products (how American was that!), but many also had religious themes. During World War II, patriotic snow globes began to appear, and the mili-tary-themed snow globes from that era are among the most coveted today.

Many of the wartime snow globes were produced by the Atlas Crystal Works, which was founded during the early 1940s by William Snyder, who wanted to honor military figures. Snyder's whole family worked together to produce the little globes. One family member stirred the liquid, another made the molds, and yet another fastened the globe to the base. Atlas became the biggest snow globe manufacturer in the country, and when the war was over, the company expanded its themes to include holidays, tourist sites, and popular figures. The business literally snowballed.

Today, many companies either manufacture or import snow globes. Of course, much about them has changed over the years. In early, more elegant days, the globe was usually glass, and the figures inside were porcelain. The "snow" consisted of any number of materials, such as ground rice, wax, or soap chips; and the base, whether round or square, might have been made of stone, marble, ceramic, or wood. Nowadays, bases are usually plastic, as is the "glass" globe. The snow is likely to be small bits of plastic.

Many people collect snow globes, and some of their collections are quite valuable. But that's not really the point. While we all appreciate the art of the more refined, delicate snow globes, it's the little palm tree with the words "The Bahamas" on the globe's base that brings out a smile as the snow incongruously stirs up lovely memories of a warm winter vacation. Snow globes are fun, silly, and completely irresistible. Come along. We think you'll enjoy our tour.

Snowy Destinations

Snow globes are not a substitute for a geography class. While some feature city skylines or beach scenes, the resemblance to the actual place pretty much stops there. Snow can materialize in Hawaii or Puerto Rico, and New York's most famous buildings can all appear to be on the same street. Reality is not the point of a snow globe—rather it's all about a sense of a place combined with the fantasies each person brings to it.

Mermaids in Puerto Rico, well, maybe—but in San Francisco?!

Famous New York buildings, including the Chrysler Building, the Twin Towers lost on September 11, the Empire State Building, and the Metropolitan Museum of Art, are all placed together in this wonderful snow globe. Beneath the globe itself is a glimpse of New York's subway, speeding under the busy streets of the metropolis. Two famous New York landmarks have their own snow globes: Rockefeller Center and Ellis Island, and at far right is a stately skyscraper.

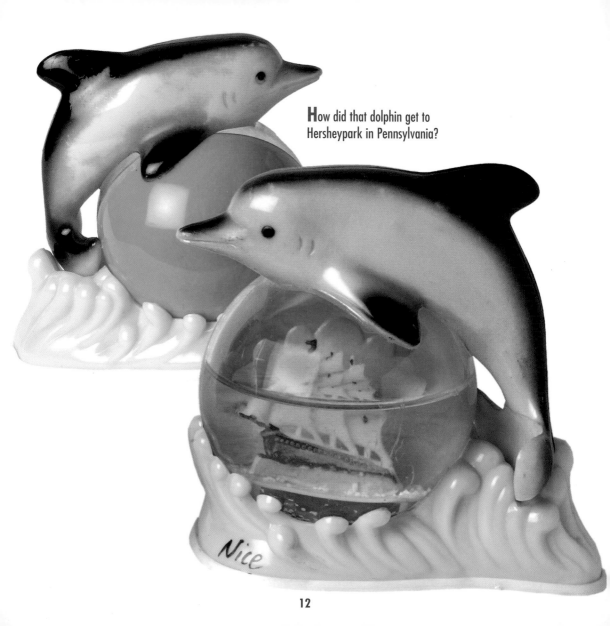

How did that dolphin get to
Hersheypark in Pennsylvania?

Nice

12

It's much safer to stay at the tourist stop and buy one of these than to look for real bears.

At right are two waterside towns that appear in bottle forms. This shape is the most popular after the globe and the flat oval. The back of the bottle is usually painted and flat.

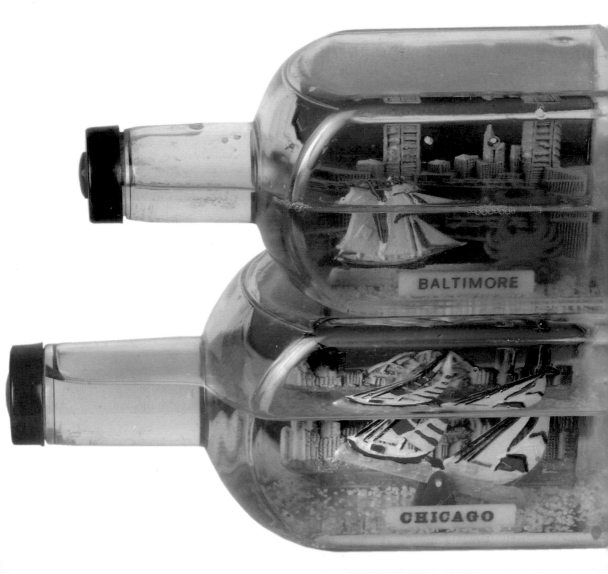

Pirates may never have found Tennessee, but it, as well as many other states, is celebrated in a priceless treasure chest.

XVAZWYVI MWEX XLT WMKR, SJ XLA WOYPP

These newly minted globes are from some of the most well-known tourist resorts. It's hard to decide whether to fly south or go skiing.

At left is winter in all its snow globe glory: a cozy cabin, a pair of penguins, and a skier.

We aren't sure that the globes on this page would really entice you to go to Florida or Louisiana—unless you are an adventurer.

The Dome: These were originally done in glass but today are almost always made of plastic. They are generally one of two shapes: round or a demi-round with a flat back. With the perpetual calendars on the base, the snow globes shown here are lifelong remembrances.

From Bloomingdale's to Betty Boop—
Hollywood is all glamour.

HOLLYWOOD

Colorado and snow—almost synonymous! What is globe snow made from? Originally from materials lying around the factory—bone chips, broken pieces of china, or wax. We understand the china but have always been puzzled as to why the bones were lying around. At any rate, today's flurries are mainly made of plastic, which holds up well to their eternal submersion.

Bases are now made of plastic and sometimes molded to suit the scene of the globe, as in the Alaska snow globe at left. More elegant globes have porcelain or china or even wood bases.

Charles Lindbergh is featured in this snow globe commemorating his historic flight. It dates from the 1930s and is quite rare. At right, St. Louis in all its 3-D glory. The Arch beautifully enfolds the city, and *The Spirit of St. Louis* is perched proudly on top of this lovely globe.

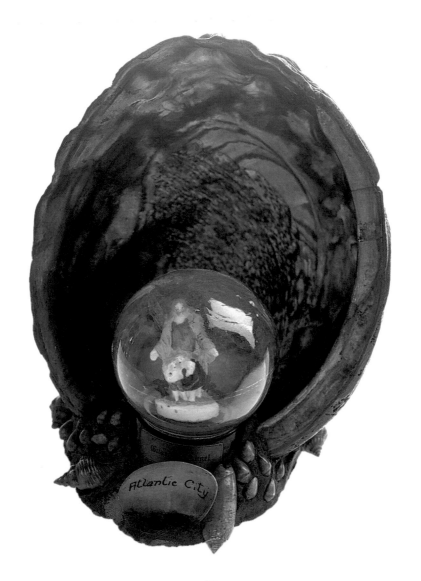

It is sometimes hard to guess how a place might be memorialized in a globe. Atlantic City's highlights a guardian angel, while Connecticut is depicted as a seafarer.

Picturesque London has inspired a large number of snow globes. The Tower Bridge globe at left is one of our favorites. The famous Italian couple at right is based on a well-known portrait by Piero della Francesca and is from Urbino, Italy.

These snow globes are not quite like the one introduced at the Paris Exposition in 1889, with its porcelain figure, ceramic snow chips, and glass dome, but if you've been to Paris and want to remember it, these will do the trick.

PARIS-TOUR-EIFFEL

Exploring Antarctica
HMS Endurance
American Museum of Natural History

At left is a tribute to Shackleton's legendary Antarctic expedition aboard the *Endurance*. To the right are penguins looking particularly at home in a snow globe.

AUSTRALIA

HOLLAND

All plastic, all corny, all recently produced; but we still feel transported.

CANADA

SHANGHAI TANG

The original Victorian-period globes had fine china or porcelain figures. Today, the figures and scenes can be made of anything that won't be affected by the liquid. Plastic is one of the most used materials. In the late 1950s and 60s, injection molding opened up the possibility for all sorts of intricate three-dimensional scenes, such as the ones shown at left and far right. Now the less expensive snow globes (such as the Jerusalem globe shown above) have flat images, which reduces production costs considerably.

Americana

Once Americans got into snow globes, they really got into snow globes. Some were produced as souvenirs of tourist destinations while others commemorated historic sites. The Atlas Crystal Works created a 1940s series that honored every branch of the armed forces. Later, Atlas produced a series of American Presidents, three of which are shown on the following pages. And of course, there is the commercial side of Americana, where products are immortalized under glass (or plastic).

The saluting admiral is a typical figural from the 1960s. Opposite, a 1942 cover of *Good Housekeeping* features a little girl mesmerized by her Santa snow globe. The tin drum snow globe at far right is an image of Sagamore Hill, the Long Island home of President Theodore Roosevelt.

USS ALABAMA

INDIAN TERRITORY

Like the admiral, this Indian is a figural from the 1960s. The boxed set at right and below by Marx has snow globes with a western theme.

Plymouth Rock 1620" is in the style of 1950s Italian snow globes, which had an enormous fondness for shell bases. "Just a Little Mammy" pictured here is part of a set that also included Little Watermelon Boy. Both were produced by Atlas in the 1940s and are an unfortunate reflection of our society at the time. Mark Twain's Hannibal, Missouri, house is charming.

MARK TWAIN'S HOME
HANNIBAL, MO.

The *Titanic* sits on a cobalt blue base and was manufactured in Germany in the 1920s. Atlas produced the bomber as part of its military series in the 1940s, and the *Nautilus* was created in the 1960s by the Driss Co. of Chicago.

STE MERE EGLISE
6 JUIN 1944

FALA

ROOSEVELT HOME
HYDE PARK, N.Y.

U.S. MILITARY ACADEMY
WEST POINT, N.Y.

At top left is a fine commemoration of the parachute drop at Sainte-Mère-Église, which was part of the World War II invasion of Normandy. Next to it is a tribute to Franklin Delano Roosevelt's house in Hyde Park, with his beloved dog Fala; the U.S. Military Academy at West Point is at bottom.

The domes on this page are tributes to Amish country and soap operas.

Atlas's series on the Presidents included Franklin Delano Roosevelt and Dwight D. Eisenhower. The Metropolitan Co. immortalized FDR's dog Fala, and Koziol of Germany created Ronald Reagan.

GENERAL
DWIGHT D. EISENHOWER
COMMANDER IN CHIEF
ALLIED INVASION FORCES

Progressive Products created the chicken on the far left to advertise its vaccine for chickens in the 1950s, while these Spam and Budweiser snow globes were homages more than advertising.

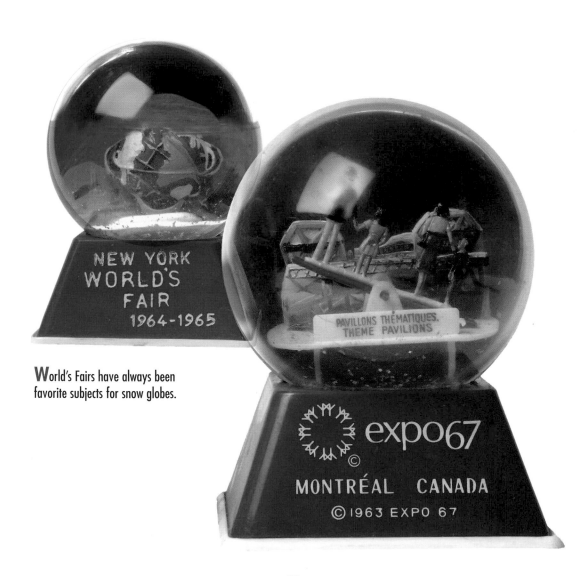

NEW YORK
WORLD'S
FAIR
1964-1965

PAVILLONS THÉMATIQUES.
THEME PAVILIONS

expo67

MONTRÉAL CANADA

©1963 EXPO 67

World's Fairs have always been
favorite subjects for snow globes.

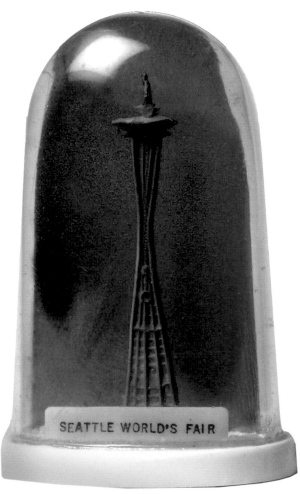

Ever forget that last-minute gift for a holiday party? Snow globes are available for the holiday of your choice, with Halloween and Christmas the most popular. The snow globe at left, with its inventive mummy's hand base, is fun and creative. At right, instead of falling snow we have swarming bats, in this creepily humorous haunted-house snow globe.

Thanksgiving inspires whimsical snow globes. The famed department store Macy's in New York City has offered several different globes that showcase its fabulous parade.

Christmas is the ideal snow globe holiday! On the following pages is a wide assortment of globes spanning several decades.

All four of these are excellent examples of figurals. The two globes on the right rock back and forth.

Both of the globes on this page are from the 1960s. The fireplace opposite is from the 1990s and was produced by Enesco. Imagine Santa's surprise when the fireplace was full of water.

These are from the 1960s as well.

The figurals on this page are from the 1960s, as is the one at near right, which is really a snow globe ornament. The far right globe rocks on its base.

Snow globes always look better than that leftover bottle of champagne when remembering New Year's Eve.

The Beasts

In the 1940s, the Atlas Crystal Works, one of the largest snow globe manufacturers, began manufacturing beautifully painted animal figures and surrounding them with glass domes. Today, even the Smithsonian Institution has its own snow globes of animal figures. A particularly fine one is the Antarctic Penguin family, which illustrates some of the globe's most exotic and breathtaking animals. As can be seen in these two globes, the animals sometimes escape their domes.

Beguiling polar bears and a nicely executed figure of a circus tiger. The base of the tiger globe ties in to the circus theme.

Underwater animals are a natural for snow globes. The Noah's Ark above is particularly interesting in that the bottom half of the globe moves when the lever is pressed. The snow globe at right is a very Florida-like scene.

With the exception of the cat on the left, which is papier-mâché, all of these globes are ceramic. There is a fish inside each of the four globes.

85

The dog was produced in the 1950s. The rest were manufactured a bit later.

Licensed Characters

Popular characters appear in collectibles from lunch boxes to PEZ dispensers to snow globes, and just about everywhere else. If you have a favorite licensed character, chances are you can find a snow globe dedicated to him, her, or it! Once you start looking, you'll see that there seem to be globes for everyone—from Felix the Cat to Elvis. Many of these globes are made in China, and one can only imagine what they conjure up about our culture. Some of the most popular have characters from the Disney Company, which began encasing Mickey and Minnie and the rest of the gang in little domes in the 1960s.

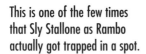

This is one of the few times that Sly Stallone as Rambo actually got trapped in a spot.

Against the backdrop of the world-famous Rockettes, this colorful snow globe commemorates one of New York City's grandest holiday traditions—the Radio City Christmas Spectacular. The Rockettes have been kicking up a storm for over 75 years, but this snow globe is considerably younger.

Many licensed characters are done in 3-D and are very appealing, especially those with fun and unusual bases. With so many snow globe manufacturers, companies started to make the bases special to distinguish their products.

Disney's snow globes are attractive and fun. Full of detail and lightheartedness, the snow globes exude a real sense of joy. Here the base is a spool of film that revolves. These mechanical bases became very popular in the 1970s. Some even play tunes. The older ones to the right take you back to simpler times in about a second.

MICKEY MOUSE

BAND CONCERT

NIFTY NIN

Harry Potter is a natural for the unnatural look of the snow globe. Shake any of the characters and they will cast a spell.

MIRROR OF ERISED

FLUFFY

POTIONS RIDDLE

The millennium even inspired Barbie. Maybe she's outside the globe so that she can keep her outfit dry and perfect.

The Addams Family house is held aloft by—of course—Hand. At right, a lovely PEZ couple stands atop their wedding cake. A little shake and the celebration begins.

Marilyn and Elvis are among the hottest stars in the snow globe world and they come in a variety of shapes and styles. Marilyn looks every inch the film star, and at left, Elvis and Elvis artifacts in all their glory.

Fargo, that quirky film from the Coen Brothers, is obviously perfect material for a snow globe. At right, snow globes at the last frontier. One commemorates the real landing on the moon. At far right, this futuristic, limited edition globe celebrates *Star Trek*, which to its ardent fans represents reality as well as NASA's discoveries do.

These fabulous globes are from Collodi,
Italy. Pinocchio is standing tall in his home-
town environment.

Below is another example of a globe from Collodi, Italy, and at right are some unusual snow globe Kleenex boxes, part of a series of eight.

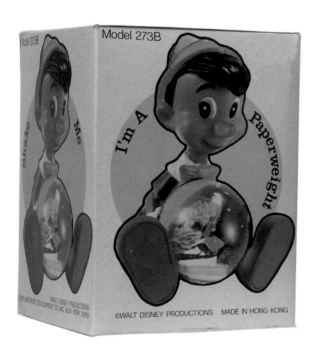

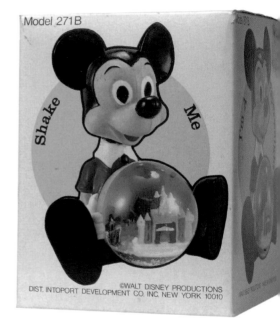

Charming examples of snow globe boxes, with
Donald Duck making a special appearance.

The prize of one collector's group of snow globes, at far left is the original 1950s Lone Ranger. At near left is Bozo from the early 1960s, and below is a recent Big Apple Circus globe.

Miscellaneous

Whatever the figure inside the globe, the real mystery remains, "What's the liquid?" Well, it has changed over the years. An early problem was that the water originally used for the liquid froze in the winter. During the 1950s, believe it or not, antifreeze was added to resolve this. Another issue was that the water became murky and polluted over time. For a while, snow globes were shipped without water and the store would add it. Now, chemicals such as glycol are added to thicken the water and make sure it doesn't freeze. These added chemicals also magnify the image and make the snow fall more slowly. The exact formulas for the ingredients in a snow globe are carefully guarded by each company's Department of Snow Globe Security.

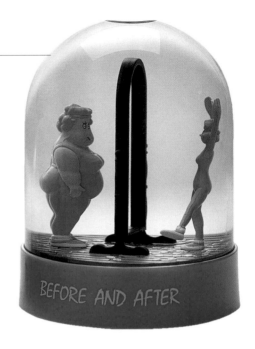

A snow globe celebrating the joys of dieting and fitness? Or just a magical mirror? At right, the daring bicyclist is a classic three-dimensional figure.

This early design TV (flat screens are not conducive to snow globes) comes complete with snacks on top to make viewing more fun. At right, flying money, not snow, is brought to you by the magic of plastics.

Snow globes are rarely political, but here are two memorable examples:
Mao Zedong at left; and above, the East/West division of Berlin.

An unusual pyramid-shaped dome. At far right, two domes from China.

A trio of rural snow globes. Past-ure Prime? makes mooing noises when you shake it.

123

Fun snow globes made with kids in mind. The teapot-shaped globe at right provides great atmosphere for this European cartoon character.

Above is one of the largest globes (the judge's dome is 8 inches tall), while at right are some of the smallest figures to be found in a globe.

Two globes commemorating Cleveland's
Rock and Roll Hall of Fame.

ROCK AND ROLL HALL OF FAME FOUNDATION

129

The Henry Moore—like sculpture at upper left, the Sphinx in the middle, and Robert Indiana's LOVE are all part of a limited edition series on great art by Don Celender. The takeoff on Salvador Dali's *Persistence of Memory* on the far right was not part of this series.

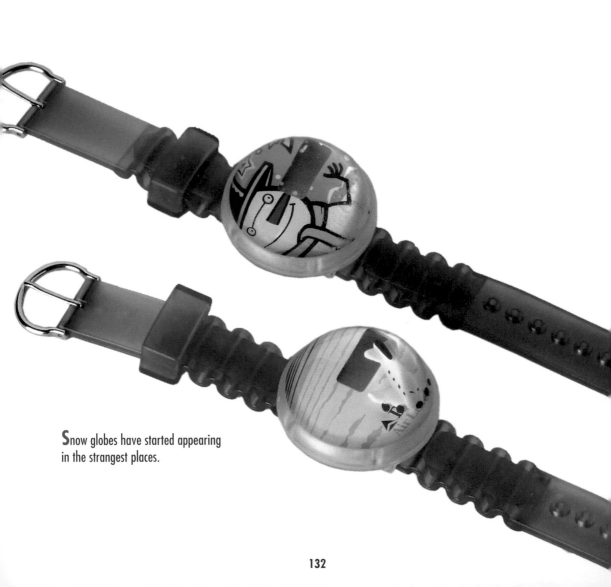

Snow globes have started appearing in the strangest places.

Religious themes have been very important throughout the years in snow globe images.

Several globes were done in honor of Popes. John Paul II, at bottom left, is from a series by the Koziol Company.

The exceptional snow globe at far left was made in Italy and represents the Sanctuary of Montenero outside of Livorno and Our Lady of Montenero. On this page is a 1980s globe representing the flight from Egypt. Below is a depiction of the Crucifixion, and another features a nun; both are from the 1960s.

Bethlehem

CRUCIFIXION

It wouldn't be an American art form if it didn't include sports. Snow globe companies have made deals with every major team here and in many other parts of the world. All of the major stadiums have their own globes. The globe at far right commemorates the Baseball Hall of Fame at Cooperstown, New York.

BASEBALL HALL OF FAME
COOPERSTOWN N.Y.

Celebrating Our Collectors

We are grateful to Mitchell Gordon and Nancy McMichael for allowing us to photograph a small part of their astonishing collections, and for providing us with so much fascinating information about snow globes.

Mitchell Gordon is a New York–based snow globe collector. He received his first one in 1983 from his wife. Many of his others were gifts from friends and colleagues. When not dusting his 2,000 snow globes, he serves as president of an investment banking firm.

Nancy McMichael, an avid snow globe collector, is an expert on their history. Most of the vintage snow globes pictured in this book belong to her. She is the author of the authoritative book *Snowdomes* and for twelve years wrote and published "Snow Biz, the Newsletter for Snowdome Collectors." Nancy collected over 6,000 domes, until her Washington, D.C., home began to sink.

The following books were instrumental in the writing of this book:

Snowdomes, by Nancy McMichael, Abbeville Press, 1990.

Snow Globes—The Collector's Guide to Selecting, Displaying, and Restoring Snow Globes, by Connie A. Moore and Harry L. Rinker, Courage Books, 1993.

Barbara J. Morgan Publisher
Leonard Vigliarolo Design Director
Robert Milazzo Photography
Jane F. Neighbors Copy Editor
Gina Graham Editorial Assistant
James Trimarco Art Assistant
Della R. Mancuso Production